TRUE
SURVIVAL
STORIES

TRUE SURVIVAL STORIES

Jack Monroe

Illustrated by
David Wyatt

Hippo

WARNING
In the Survivalist's Handbook sections of this book you will find
some useful and interesting information about how to survive in
the wild. But remember that you should never go out into the wild
alone, without expert guidance and proper equipment, and that
you should abide by the laws protecting land, plants and animals
unless you are in a real emergency situation.

Scholastic Children's Books,
Scholastic Publications Ltd,
7-9 Pratt Street, London NW1 OAE, UK

Scholastic Inc.,
555 Broadway, New York, NY 10012-3999, USA

Scholastic Canada Ltd,
123 Newkirk Road, Richmond Hill,
Ontario, Canada L4C 3G5

Ashton Scholastic Pty Ltd,
P O Box 579, Gosford, New South Wales,
Australia

Ashton Scholastic Ltd,
Private Bag 94407, Greenmount, Auckland,
New Zealand

First published by Scholastic Publications Ltd, 1995

Text copyright © Jack Monroe, 1995
Illustrations copyright © David Wyatt, 1995

ISBN 0 590 55861 7

Typeset by Contour Typesetters, Southall, London
Printed by Cox & Wyman Ltd, Reading, Berks

10 9 8 7 6 5 4 3 2 1

Contents

Introduction

These stories are all about real people who showed amazing courage in life-threatening situations. Whether alone and adrift at sea, at the controls of a plummeting plane, or helping others to safety from a sinking ship, these heroes and heroines are exceptional for their bravery and determination.

Their tales, and others like them, show how easy it is for the shortest trip to turn into a nightmare – like Michelle Hamilton's holiday canoe ride that rapidly became the most terrifying ordeal of her life. It's important to remember that you should never venture out into the wild alone, without expert and experienced people and proper equipment.

Your chances of survival in the wild are better if you learn some survival techniques – how to build a shelter, find food and water, keep warm or cool depending on the conditions, and find your way. The fact sections in this book provide some basic but fascinating hints and information, and might enourage you to find out more about survival. You never know, one day this information could help to save your life.

But for now, you can experience the adventure, danger and excitement of surviving alone in the jungle, or a death-defying parachute rescue, without any of the risks! Relax in the comfort and safety of your own armchair, and prepare to read some fascinating tales of courage, self-lessness and determination.

Guardian
Angel

"**M**ayday! Mayday!" screeched the overhead speaker in the control room at Cardiff Airport in South Wales.

Air traffic controller John Hibberd automatically checked his watch as he flipped the radio switch on the control panel in front of him. It was 6.39pm, March 30, 1992. He spoke into the mike: "Mayday, go ahead."

A frightened voice crackled into his ears. "I think my pilot has had a heart attack. I haven't a clue what to do! I don't know how to fly!"

Alan Anderson, a young mechanic from South Wales, had never enjoyed flying. In fact, the very thought of it terrified him. But he hadn't wanted to admit that to his girlfriend's father, Les Rhoades.

Alan liked Les. They had been pals ever since Alison had introduced them two years before. But Alan knew he would never hear the last of it if he refused to "go for a bumble" in Les's 22-year-old plane, and he finally agreed.

Les's plane was a single-engined craft, called *Gaydog* after its official call sign "G-AYDOG".

It had been airborne for 30 minutes, heading west from Cardiff along the coast. In the passenger seat, Alan was amazed to discover that he had actually begun to enjoy himself. The cockpit was warm and comfortable. The waves of the Bristol Channel, 900 metres beneath them, were flecked gold by the westering sun. Beside him, Les was quietly humming as he nursed the tiny plane into a wide turn, the dual control stick between Alan's legs faithfully repeating each of Les's actions.

Alan breathed happily. This is brilliant, he thought. It's like flying with my guardian angel.

After 30 minutes or so, they turned back towards Cardiff. "Let's chase that cloud," suggested Les, nodding towards a lone cloud up ahead.

"Do we have to, Les? It's bad enough just being up here," joked Alan.

But there was no response. Les had stopped humming. His head fell slowly forward. His fingers lost their grip on the control stick and his arms flopped to his sides. *Gaydog*'s nose tilted gently towards the ground.

Ha! Ha! Good joke, Les, thought Alan.

But Les didn't stir as *Gaydog*'s nose dipped still further into a steeper and steeper dive.

"Come on, Les, stop messing around," urged Alan into the radio headset he had been wearing since take-off. "I'm getting scared."

But Les still didn't move.

Alan was forced to press his body harder and harder into the back of his seat as the plane began to drop out of the sky ... 600 metres ... 450 metres ... 300 metres. Feverishly, he fumbled inside Les's jacket for a heartbeat. There was nothing.

Frozen with fear, crushed into the back of his seat, Alan stared through the windscreen. The ground seemed to be rushing up towards them ... streets ... roofs ... cars ... factory buildings. They were hurtling straight for three enormous chimney stacks. With a despairing sob, Alan grabbed at the dual control stick in front of him and wrenched it towards his stomach. *Gaydog* began a steep climb. The plane missed crashing into the chimneys by seconds.

"Help! Help! Mayday!" Alan screamed into his headset. No one answered. He felt beads of cold sweat trickling down his brow. A jumble of wild, unrelated thoughts raced through his mind.

Oh God, what am I going to do now? How am I going to tell Alison about her father? I wonder if she knows how much I love her? What am I going to do? What am I going to do?

He pushed the control stick away from him. As long as he clung to it the plane flew steadily and level.

"Help! Help! Mayday!" he sobbed again and again into his headset. Still no one answered. In his panic, he realized that there was something different about Les's headset. He removed it with fumbling fingers, and put it on.

Again he screamed: "Mayday! Mayday!" But there was still nothing. Shakily he gripped the control column harder. For some reason – perhaps by accident, perhaps in an automatic reflex action – he pressed the button on the top of the stick. "Mayday!" he repeated. Suddenly, his headphones crackled into life.

"Mayday, go ahead," said a quiet, comforting voice in his ears. Thank God! Thank God! breathed Alan.

Air traffic controller John Hibberd had been trained to handle the sort of crisis he was now facing. Yet he still felt a shiver of fear run through his body as the voice in his headphones confirmed: "I don't know how to fly."

"How is the pilot?"

"He's cold, I think he's had a heart attack," said Alan's shaky voice.

Hibberd had already checked his radar screen. It told him that *Gaydog* was to the west of the airport. But so were four other aircraft. Which one was Alan's?

"Can you look at the dials ahead of you and see what heading you are on?" he asked.

The eye-level compass directly in front of Alan was unmistakable. "Number 12, next to the east," he read aloud.

"That's fine," Hibberd located *Gaydog* on his screen. "You're heading directly back to the airport," he said, before temporarily breaking voice contact in order to warn other aircraft to keep clear.

Alan clung to the control stick. He felt deserted. Where's he gone, where's he gone, where's he gone? he kept repeating to himself. It seemed ages since Hibberd had last spoken.

Why doesn't he tell me how he's going to help me?

He can't help me. I'm going to die!

I'll never manage to land!

Alan thought wildly that he could head for the Bristol Channel where he could crash the aircraft when it ran out of fuel. Before it hit the water he would unstrap Les and jump with him into the sea.

But then, 500 metres below, no bigger than the top of a coffee table, he spotted Cardiff Airport. He pressed the radio button:

"Cardiff Airport, I'm just coming over the runway now."

Air traffic controller Colin Eaton, an RAF veteran, had been taking a tea break when an urgent call for his assistance was relayed from the radar room. He raced back and, out of breath, eased himself into his seat. Next to him, Hibberd was talking to the pilot of another light aircraft who had radioed in to offer assistance – Robert Legg.

Few people could have been better qualified to help. Robert Legg was only 26, the same age as Alan, yet he was already an experienced flying instructor. He had been flying some five miles north of Cardiff airport, with a student, when he heard the drama aboard *Gaydog* unfolding over his earphones.

Colin Eaton hastily radioed to the terrified Alan: "This is the air traffic controller . . . There is an aircraft about four miles to the west of you. He is rapidly approaching you to draw alongside, and then he will be speaking to you on this frequency.'

On a surge of adrenalin, Legg turned his aircraft – *Charlie Echo* in radio speak – and began searching the skies for *Gaydog*. He spotted the plane some 300 metres below them and put *Charlie Echo* into a full power dive, at the same time radioing Alan to tell him he was coming up behind.

"If you look to your right, just behind your wing, you may see my aircraft," announced Legg's voice in Alan's headset. Alan swivelled his head, pressing his face hard against the cockpit canopy. There's nothing there! he thought. Frantically, he searched the skies. "I'll get you down as quickly as possible," said the confident voice in his ears.

In reality, Legg had no idea how he would achieve this. One thing at a time, he told himself firmly.

He spoke soothingly into his mike. "Hold the control column in front of you. Rotate it gently to the right and put the aircraft into a bank turn to the right. We're going to circle over the airfield in a nice wide circuit and then we're going to bring you down on to the runway."

At Cardiff airport, 600 metres below them, full emergency drill had been put into action. Fire crews were positioned along the runway. The local county fire brigade headquarters had been alerted, as had the police and the ambulance service. An RAF Tristar tanker had been ordered to stay clear of the airspace, and an incoming passenger aircraft had been put into a holding pattern.

In the radar room, John Hibberd had been listening to Legg's calm, precise instructions. "This guy's good," he muttered to Colin Eaton.

In the air, Robert Legg coolly calculated the chances of getting Alan down alive. He realized they were slim. For a start, Alan was going much too fast for a landing approach. Robert told him to ease out the throttle.

"Which one is the throttle?" asked Alan.

In the radar room, Colin Eaton turned to Hibberd in horror. "Good grief," he breathed. "If he gets down it will be a miracle!"

Although he was shaken by Alan's response, Robert Legg forced himself to remain calm. Gently, patiently, he told Alan how to reduce the aircraft's speed. "Now, ease back on the control column to maintain your altitude."

Gaydog slowed to 100 mph (160 kph) as Robert nursed his own aircraft closer and closer. Soon, he was flying just a couple of hundred metres to Alan's left.

"I can see you!" exclaimed Alan. Remembering a scene from the film *Airport 1975*, he waited eagerly for signs that the other aircraft was being manoeuvred closer so that the pilot could jump on board and take over the controls.

He'll land it for me, he thought.

But Robert Legg was a professional pilot. He knew there is a world of difference between what is possible in films and what can be achieved in real life. Alan had to land *Gaydog* himself – and as a complete novice, his chances were next to nil. The odds Robert gave for Alan's chances of survival were a million to one!

Hang on, hang on, muttered Robert, forcing himself to think clearly. He knows the basics now, using the throttle and control stick . . . but all he's done is make a right turn . . . it's not enough!

He spoke soothingly into his mike. "We're going to fly over the runway first."

In despair, Alan realized there was going to be no miraculous mid-air rescue. *I'm going to die!* he thought. There was no way he could land the aircraft on his own. Why can't someone help me? he wanted to scream. Aloud, he asked Robert if there was anyone who would contact Alison and tell her about Les.

Robert Legg recognized the panic-stricken tremor in Alan's voice. He's close to cracking, he thought. Gently but firmly he ordered, "Just concentrate on my instructions. We're going to do a left-hand circuit . . . a nice gentle turn to the left about the same sort of rate as we did before . . . and we're going to come all the way round again and bring the plane down on the runway. Do you understand?"

Alan forced himself to concentrate. "Yeah," he gulped. "I understand. But how do you stop it?"

Robert Legg ignored the question. "Hold the aircraft in a gentle turn . . . That's fine. Add a little more power. Pull slightly back on the control column to maintain your height."

Gaydog completed a left-hand circuit above the airfield. The runway was now dead ahead, about 120 metres below them. It still seemed very small. Maybe I can make it if I land on the grass, Alan thought.

"This time I'm going to attempt to get you down," said Robert's voice. "Just aim for the runway . . . just a gentle bank left . . . as you've done before."

The plane was now about two kilometres from the airport runway, which looked no bigger than a grey splinter of glinting tarmac in the distance. Alan knew he was going to crash. But there were three things on his side: the plane he was flying handled well at low speeds, there was very little wind, and although the runway looked tiny, it had been designed to take giant 747 passenger airliners.

This is it, thought Alan, as *Gaydog* floated down 30 metres. Either I do this or I die!

"I'd like you to slightly reduce the throttle," said the voice in his headset. "Come over to the right a little . . . we're aiming for the big tarmac strip to the right of the white and red lights."

The plane was over the beginning of the runway. Alan concentrated hard, religiously translating Robert's words into actions: "Pull the throttle all the way towards you now and pull gently back on the control column . . . Hold it there . . . Hold it . . ."

Gaydog's nose dipped. The runway seemed to rise up. It filled the windscreen, hurtling itself at the tiny plane. There was a gentle lurch as Alan made a perfect landing.

"He's made it!" shouted an ecstatic Colin Eaton in the radar room.

But Alan's eyes were still clamped tightly shut. He braced himself as *Gaydog* coasted on down the runway, expecting at any moment to crash into parked planes. But his guardian angel had not deserted him. The plane veered on to the grass and rolled gently to a halt.

As air traffic controller John Hibberd commented later: "Someone up there was clearly looking out for Alan Anderson that day!" A lot of people say that Alan's guardian angel was Robert Legg. Members of the Royal Aero Club agree; they awarded him a silver medal for achievement in aviation. But Robert claims his actions were merely "all in a day's work"!

Postscript: Poor Les Rhoades had suffered a massive heart attack. He was pronounced dead on arrival at hospital, where Alan was treated for shock and then released. Not long afterwards, he and Alison announced their engagement. Although he swore he would never fly again, Alan overcame his fears and, as a tribute to Les, went up in *Gaydog* once more – with a pilot – just four months after his ordeal.

The Survivalist's Handbook

Chapter 1:

Shelter and Warmth

I magine you are lost miles from anywhere, in cold, wet weather, with no
obvious source of shelter and warmth.
You don't know how long it might be before
help arrives. What do you do? How will you
keep warm and dry?

1.   The best form of warmth and shelter in
the wild is yourself, your friends and your
clothes. You and your friends, because by
curling up together you can share each
other's life-saving body heat. Your clothes,
because they can insulate you against
extreme temperatures.

2.   Did you know that you generate the
heat of a 100-watt light bulb? It's important
not to let any of that heat escape. Suitable
clothing is essential: a hat, as a fifth of your
body heat is lost through your head; waterproof shoes or boots, worn with thick socks;
and a waterproof and windproof jacket and
trousers. Layers of clothing make good
insulation.

3.   If you're going to be in the desert, make
sure you cover up as much of your body as
possible, to protect it from the sun. Because
of the heat, clothing needs to be lightweight

and porous. Eyes also need protecting from the sun – wear good quality sunglasses if possible, otherwise make sure your face is shaded. In the jungle, cover up completely to prevent insect bites. Strong, lightweight clothing is needed, and a hat with a mosquito net, but waterproof clothing will make you sweat.

4. A survival bag is essential if you're going to be in remote or difficult conditions. "Bivi bags" weigh hardly anything at all, but they provide amazing protection against the elements in extreme cold – two bags, one inside the other, with the gap between them filled with grass or ferns, can keep you surprisingly warm.

5. If you're caught out in the wild alone, look for some form of shelter – you'll need a space just big enough for you to get into, so that your body heats the air around you as quickly as possible. Roll up into a ball to keep warm. You could build a lean-to "bivouac" quite easily, but even a large rock, a tree or a fallen log will provide basic protection.

6. Ferns, bracken, reeds, grass, heather, pine needles, or anything similar you can lay your hands on, will help conserve heat. You could line your shelter with any or all of these, a bit like a bird's nest.

Survival is all very well, but in reality you're going to want to be found! Take a whistle and a torch with you, and your rescuers will reach you all the sooner.

Lost in
the Jungle

There is a saying among the people of Gabon on the north-western coast of Africa: 'When the jungle takes you, it doesn't let go.'

Only someone who has been lost within the dense, suffocating half-light and heat of the equatorial jungle can fully appreciate the truth of that Gabonese saying – someone like 66-year-old Doctor Leoncio Bravo Salvador, 'Salva' to his friends and family.

There were just four days of Salva's African holiday left. After two weeks driving over the red dust jungle and savannah tracks of south-east Gabon, he and his family were heading for civilization in the nearest town, Franceville. There they were to stay with their friend Jérome Okinda, Gabon's Minister of Health, before flying home to the south of France.

It was hot, a sweltering 50°C. Salva's wife Claire, 30 years younger than him, had wanted to drive the remaining 22 miles to Franceville without stopping. She and their young son Christian were tired. But Salva wanted them to see the great waterfalls of Chutes de Poubara, which he had last visited 20 years earlier when he was medical officer at Okondja, a village north of Franceville.

"It is too good an opportunity to miss. You must see the falls," he had insisted. "There's plenty of time."

At about 3.30pm on Wednesday 6 November, they parked their car near the jungle village of Poubara, a kraal[1] of native huts on the edge of the River Ogooue. With a small boy as their guide, they crossed a rickety, swinging bridge woven from *lianas*, the name Gabonese natives use for all climbing and twining vines in the jungle.

1. South African hut village.

The boy pointed upstream to the trail they would take through the jungle. But Salva, a keen photographer, wanted a high vantage point for his pictures of the falls. He was at the rear of the group and, without a word, he left them, looking for a higher trail through the jungle. It was a stupid thing to do.

Only when they were getting near to the falls did Claire realize Salva wasn't behind her. "Typical!" she muttered. But she wasn't worried; Salva was small, but he was wiry and tough and knew how to look after himself. As a younger man he had often gone on safari, visiting lost native tribes in the jungles of West Africa. He had even survived bombs and bullets when he was a field surgeon during the Biafran civil war. She fully expected her husband to catch up when they reached the falls.

Meanwhile, Salva was pushing his way deeper and deeper into the jungle. He was already disorientated. Suddenly he felt a blinding flash of pain in his head. His legs collapsed beneath him. Before his body hit the ground he caught a glimpse of two pairs of legs. A second blow on the back of his head sent him spinning into unconsciousness.

Meanwhile, Claire was unable to enjoy the beauty of Chutes de Poubara, where the River Ogooue plunges dramatically over a gigantic rock step. Peering into the boiling turmoil of froth, she grew increasingly worried that Salva had failed to join them. Had he slipped and fallen in?

"Salva! Salva!" she shouted. But the thunderous roar of the mighty falls threw the words back into her face.

Claire grew close to panic. It was nearly an hour since Salva had disappeared without a word. She and Christian returned the way they had come, searching every inch of the trail. There was no sign of her husband anywhere. As she entered the village, looking for a phone, a violent storm broke out. I hope Salva is taking shelter somewhere, she thought.

In the jungle, Salva awoke, wet and cold. There was a pain in his ribs, blood trickled down the side of his face, his head was swollen, and a loud and unceasing roar in his ears told him that his skull was almost certainly fractured. Weakly, he shook his head and gently massaged his ears, but he could hear nothing beyond the cacophony of sound raging inside his head; the attack had left him totally deaf. He lost consciousness again.

There was no telephone in the village. Holding Christian's hand for comfort, Claire hiked to a hydroelectric power station further down the Ogooue river. Jean-Claude Humez, the station manager, helped her to ring Jérome Okinda in Franceville to raise the alarm. Then, accompanied by Humez, and despite the oncoming darkness and soaking rain, she searched the area again. In Franceville, meanwhile, Okinda was alerting the authorities with instructions that they were to initiate a search around the area of the falls at first light the following morning.

The rain continued throughout most of that night. Claire found sleep impossible. It's raining so hard he'll be chilled to the bone, she thought. There was no doubt in her mind that, somewhere, somehow, Salva was alive.

The next day, while police combed the area, she borrowed a small plane from a local flying club and flew sweep-searches over the jungle. How long can a man survive in that? she wondered.

Slowly, Salva regained consciousness. In the dim half-light of the jungle, where daylight never penetrates through the trees, he gently rubbed life back into his aching body. His camera was gone, his wallet had been emptied, he couldn't hear anything. But he still had his watch, hidden by the long sleeves of his shirt. It was 8am on Friday 8 November. It had been 4pm on Wednesday when he left Claire and Christian. He had been unconscious for 40 hours.

He peered into the jungle, barely able to see in the gloom. His ribs were in agony and the roaring sound in his head made him frantic. He thought he could see venomous mambas and rhinoceros vipers squirming through the inch-thick lianas which surrounded him; a single bite from their fangs could kill a man in just 15 minutes. He remembered the region's bloodsucking tsetse flies that brought with them sleeping sickness and a lingering death.

It would be so easy just to curl up and die, he thought. He felt guilty about the way he had just slipped away from Claire and Christian and about the worry he must be causing them. They're waiting for me, he said to himself. I mustn't give up.

He had a raging thirst and hunger pangs. There were clusters of berries hanging from thick fronds of jungle plants; they might have helped stave off his thirst and ease the pain of hunger, but Salva's medical knowledge made him wary of eating plants and berries which might be poisonous.

Staggering to his feet, he began fighting a path through the dense liana vines. The undergrowth quickly reduced his shirt and trousers to tatters, branches and the jagged edges of lianas lashed and lacerated his hands and face, and in no time he was covered from head to foot in blood and cuts. He had no idea which way he had come, which way safety lay.

After hours of painful battling, it seemed nothing short of a miracle when Salva saw light ahead of him. Eventually, he emerged on to the open savannah and looked around. In the distance, overhead, was a light aircraft. He waved frantically, but it turned away. By now it was late afternoon and a roasting heat haze still shimmered off the dry brown earth. His tongue was swollen and the saliva inside his mouth had turned to glue. He returned into the shade on the edge of the jungle and slept.

When Salva woke that evening, the search for water took him back into the jungle. He found a rough path marked by elephant tracks, leading to a watering-hole. He drank as much water as possible, crouched at the edge of the muddy hole like a cat alert for danger, his eyes striving to pierce the darkness. He was still totally deaf.

Later on that night he drank again, determined to fill his body with as much liquid as possible. Satiated, he rocked back on his heels and found himself surrounded by an eerie wall of blue lights. They were the eyes of big toads, watching him intently. He knew that the night must be full of their croaking chorus, yet he could hear nothing.

For the first time, he began to plan his survival. He decided to hide in the jungle at night and reappear on the savannah in daytime when there was a vague chance of being spotted from the air. He began to draw on the bush knowledge acquired during his earlier years in Africa.

He decided that every evening he would stuff leaves into what was left of his tattered shirt, keeping him warm against the sharp drop in temperature of the tropical night. The padding would also help to protect him from snake bites.

He recalled another trick he had learnt from native tribesmen. They would embalm themselves in mud as a protection against the vicious tsetse flies and mosquitoes which, with a single bite, could cause malaria and death. Before moving away from the water hole that morning, Salva rolled in its mud, like a hippopotamus. A good coating should also help protect my skin against the sun, he figured.

Then he made his way out of the jungle before trekking north, the way the plane had gone. Sticking out of his mouth, and bent so that it veiled his face, was a large jungle fern, while smaller ones poked out from his ears like feathers – another native ruse intended to protect his face against tiny black flies which threatened to swarm into his nose, mouth and ears, leaving parasites that could blind.

The next day was Sunday, and the first time Claire had not joined the search party. Instead she tried to rest at Okinda's home in Franceville. Reluctantly, she began to think of a future without Salva.

"Don't cry, Maman," Christian would say to her.

But Claire knew that time was running out.

At dawn on Tuesday, day six of his ordeal, Salva awoke with a start. With his eyes clamped shut he felt the warm, breathing tickle of an elephant's trunk brush across his face. He felt a fanning breeze as the elephant flapped its ears above him. Before he had made up his mind whether to jump to his feet or play dead, he felt the ground tremble as the animal plodded away into the jungle. He shuddered at the thought of those crushing feet passing just inches away from his head.

Out on the savannah he tried to fix his bearings, singling out a distant acacia tree where he would make the day's first rest stop. He reached it with a sense of elation – there were human foot prints close to the base of the tree. But, with a heart-wrenching shock, he realized they were his own, made sometime the day before, or even the day before that. He was going round in circles! You're cracking up, he told himself in disgust. *You must hang on.*

Fixing his eyes firmly on a range of distant hills, he trudged on.

On day seven, Salva was once again woken from his slumbers with a start. A warm tongue was licking him! He reached out and touched a hairy snout. There was a loud snort. He scrambled to his feet and watched a wart-hog trotting off. He could hear its indignant squeals.

It's a miracle, he thought. I can hear! I'm not deaf any more! Claire, Claire, don't give up on me!

Before nightfall he saw in the far distance a plantation of cultivated conifers. *Civilization!* But he was now weak from hunger. That night he found no water-holes. Parched with thirst, he felt on the brink of insanity. So close to safety, so far away from rescue.

Claire had moved to Libreville. "You must go home," Okinda persuaded her. "I'll look after things here." She was beginning to face the terrible probability that she would never see Salva again.

Her flight to France was scheduled for 11.20pm, but due to an air strike it was delayed for 24 hours. That night, Claire cried herself to sleep.

*   *   *

Now close to delirium, Salva was trapped on the eighth day in a deep gorge just metres from the conifer plantation. He thought he could hear the sounds of traffic. Six times he had tried to climb out of the rocky gorge, six times he slipped back to the bottom. Finally, his strength ebbing away, he managed to cling to a liana half-way up. He worked his way higher, but a wall of lianas prevented him going any higher.

This is it, this is where it is going to end, he thought. Suddenly he heard voices. "Help," he croaked weakly. "Is anybody there?" The voices had gone. "Is anybody there? I am Salvador!"

"It's Dr Salvador!" came a triumphant shout. "Where are you? Can you climb up?"

"I can't."

"Then keep calling. We'll find you."

He heard them cutting their way towards him. He could hear the swish of their machete blades . . . closer . . . closer . . . he saw the sunlight glint on a steel blade. Two burly Gabonese, their faces streaming with sweat, slashed their way through the final cordon of lianas. Open-mouthed, they stared down at Salva.

He looked thin and old, an apparition plastered from head to toe in a thick crust of dark brown mud. But behind his mud-encrusted beard he was grinning from ear to ear.

The men helped him out of the gorge and then carried him three miles through the conifer plantation to a road where they hitched a ride to Franceville. They fed him on mangoes, his first food in eight days. Doctors at the Franceville hospital shook their heads in disbelief when they saw him. He had lost 10 kilograms, two of his ribs were broken, and his face, hands, arms and legs were raw from cuts and bruises, although the mud appeared to have acted as a healing agent. His survival was declared a miracle.

Immediately he heard the wonderful news, Okinda rang Claire in Libreville. He could hardly speak for emotion. "Claire," he choked. "Salva's alive."

Some time later, Claire and Christian walked into Salva's hospital ward. He was propped up in bed, his arm attached to a drip-feed. He held out his hand.

"Forgive me, Claire," he muttered, through a mist of tears. "It was all my fault."

The Survivalist's Handbook

Chapter 2:

Finding Water

People have been known to survive without food for over a month, but no one can live for more than ten days without water. And to survive in very hot conditions, we need water at least every two or three days. So it's vital for the survivalist to know some simple ways of finding drinkable water in the wild.

1. You should drink only the purest and cleanest water you can find, and even then the water should be filtered and boiled. Bear in mind that the further you go from the source of water, the greater the risk that it could be dirty: a clear-looking mountain stream could have a dead animal lying across it a couple of kilometres upstream.

2. All water found in the wild needs to be strained through a filter. A tightly-woven cloth is a simple filter, but a better method is to pass the water through clean gravel and sand. Alternatively, you can dig a pit about one and a half metres from the edge of a stream, and let water from the stream seep into it, filtering through the earth in between. But best of all, use one of the simple filter bags available from camping supply shops, if you've come prepared!

3.   All water should be boiled furiously for at least five minutes. If you're on high ground you'll need to boil the water for longer, because at higher altitudes water boils at lower temperatures.

4.   Rain is an obvious source of fresh water, and one which should not need filtering or purifying. But because the air can be polluted, it's best to boil rain water before drinking it. The same goes for snow and ice, which should be melted first anyway – suck snow or ice without melting them and you could end up with stomach cramps.

5.   Even at the seaside fresh water may not be far away – you can find it behind sand dunes. Rain water seeps down to the foot of a dune, and floats to the top of any sea water that might have filtered through from the sea.

6.   All survival books will tell you never to drink sea water – or urine, in case you're ever tempted! – but you can make a 'desalination unit', which turns sea water into fresh, drinkable water. To do this, you need to boil the salt water in an open container and drape a cloth over the top. When the water boils, the cloth will become saturated with fresh water from the steam. Squeeze the water from the cloth (once it's cooled down, of course), and it is drinkable.

7. Animals are much better at finding water than people are. A swarm of wild bees is never very far from fresh water; you could follow a steady stream of bees flying to their water source. A single file of ants climbing a tree is often on its way to a supply of fresh water in a hollow of the tree. Also, the tracks of grazing animals will eventually lead to water – especially if the tracks lead down-hill.

8. Plants can be a good source of water, too. Some, like the pitcher plant, fill up with rainwater to trap insects. The prickly pear, a type of cactus, stores water in its fleshy leaves, which can be chewed for their moisture. Many plants, especially those found in very hot countries, such as the acacia and banana tree, store water in their roots. But remember, plants should only be damaged and used for their water in an emergency. And, again, all water found in the wild should be filtered and boiled before you drink it.

Of course, if you are going to be outdoors, away from towns or villages, it is best to carry as much water as you need for your trip. Each person should take at least two litres of water for every day away from a water source, with some extra in reserve.

The Miracle
of the
Oceanos

There is an enduring seafaring custom known as the Birkenhead Drill – 'women and children first' – in honour of the British troop carrier *HMS Birkenhead* which hit a reef in 1852. Fearing that the life-boats carrying women and children would be swamped, the commanding officer asked his men to "Stand fast!" Not a man moved . . . 445 of them went down with the ship.

But on the evening of Saturday, August 3, 1991, when the passenger liner *Oceanos* set sail on her fateful voyage from the Buffalo River harbour in South Africa, not one of the ship's senior officers was to honour the Birkenhead Drill.

The *Oceanos* was a giant of a ship: 150 metres long, six decks tall, weighing 12,000 tonnes. She was 39 years old, no longer in the prime of life, but she was luxuriously appointed and carried the highest possible safety rating from Lloyd's Register of Shipping.

There were 571 people on board when *Oceanos* nosed her way out of the harbour entrance to head north towards Durban, some 435 kilometres up the treacherous east coast of Africa. There were 361 passengers, and 184 crew members, 6 administrators and, finally, 20 ship's entertainers, employed to organize the social whirl which passengers expected on their fair-weather holiday cruises.

"The passengers are on holiday," cruise director Lorraine Betts told her team of administrators and entertainers. "You're here to work." The group smiled back at her grimly; they had entertained a large wedding party in harbour the previous day and had only managed to catnap during the past 48 hours. Now, without pause, the revelry was due to start all over again.

It was 8pm that night when the *Oceanos* began to pitch and roll in the huge waves whipped up by a 40-knot wind. Below decks, passengers playing slot machines in the ship's casino were thrown across the room as the deck slipped away from under their feet. From the next door lounge there was a cry of "Watch out!" as the grand piano crashed from the stage.

"I think we're in for a rough time," one passenger remembers saying to his wife.

A ship's musician, Tracy Hills, was dozing fitfully in her cabin, catching up on lost sleep. Suddenly, an ear-splitting crash woke her. Heavy cabin trunks had been tossed across the room and smashed against the wall. There was a dense curtain of white foam boiling at the closed porthole; suddenly, water spurted through the seal, soaking everything in the cabin.

Outside the door, her husband, Moss, was about to put his key in the lock when three agitated ship's security officers staggered past him along the passageway. Curious, he followed. Outside a door marked 'Generator Room', oil-smeared crew members were dripping water all over the floor, yelling at each other at the tops of their voices.

Then the entire ship was plunged into total darkness as a dull explosion sent a tremor through the vessel. The *Oceanos* lay dead in the water, rolling and slewing sideways in the enormous swells. The emergency generator cut in, throwing eerie, half-light shadows everywhere.

The deck officers were huddled on the bridge, white-faced. Captain Yiannis Avranas, still dressed in his tropical whites, looked stunned, haggard, no longer the cool and dashing figure he had cut earlier in the day. His officers were staring at him in nervous silence. The staff captain was shouting over and over again into the radio: "Mayday . . . Mayday . . . Mayday . . . "

The door to the bridge burst open, bringing with it the howling sounds of a raging gale. The chief engineer staggered in, stuttering with shock and fear, already wearing a life-jacket and clutching a duffel bag to his chest. "H-h-h-hull plates have fractured on the starboard side," he stammered breathlessly. "The watertight doors won't stop the flooding."

"Oh, my God," muttered Avranas. In stunned silence he struggled to come to terms with the fact that there was nothing to stop the sea pouring through the web of drainage pipes, surging from outlets all over the ship, gradually flooding the vessel deck by deck. In no time at all the build up of water in the bows would drag her down.

"How fast is the water coming in?" he barked.

"We only have a few hours." The chief engineer swung on his heels and raced off the bridge.

"The crew knows we're sinking," reported a breathless deck officer. "They're abandoning ship."

Bewildered, Avranas looked around him. Officers who had been standing on the bridge only minutes before had already slipped away. The captain shrugged and hurried to his cabin. "Get dressed," he told his wife and their four-year-old daughter. "We're in trouble."

One of the ship's magicians, Robin Boltman, was on his way to the main lounge when members of the crew rushed past him. He tumbled after them up on to the lifeboat deck, and his jaw dropped at what he saw. A jostling, screaming crowd of fully-dressed officers and crew were piling into a lifeboat.

Back in the lounge he relayed the news to Lorraine Betts. "Let them go, we don't need scared people around," she declared. Then she hurried off to confront the captain.

"What's happening?" she demanded. Avranas would not meet her eyes. "How serious is the situation, Captain?" she asked firmly.

"Everyone must gather in the main lounge. Tell your staff to fetch life-jackets from below," he answered.

Lorraine hurried below. Can he handle the situation? she wondered. He already seems a bundle of nerves. Don't say he's buckling under the strain.

She mustered her staff – singers, dancers, musicians, cabaret artistes and hostesses. "Quiet!" she ordered the chattering, nervous group. "The captain says we have engine trouble. There's been some flooding below. Nothing serious. Go to each cabin and tell everyone to assemble for lifeboat drill in the main lounge. No passengers are allowed back below. Bring all the life-jackets and blankets you can find. No questions!" she declared as a babble of voices broke out around her. "Just do as I say."

Soon, hundreds of passengers, many in jeans and T-shirts, others in suits and cocktail dresses, a handful dressed only in flimsy night clothes, were sitting in the gloomy lounge. Robin Boltman, the magician, was climbing on to the stage.

"Sorry about the lights, folks. We forgot to pay the bill," he joked. "May I have your attention, please."

The passengers stirred. John and Gail Adamson, who had taken the trip to celebrate their eleventh wedding anniversary, squatted on the floor, tying on their children's life-jackets with trembling fingers. Only 17 days before, Gail had given birth to a son; the baby, together with his two sisters, aged eight and two, were on board with them. John looked at his wife. Whatever's gone wrong, it can't be all that bad, he told himself. Passenger liners don't sink, not in this day and age.

A hostess leaned over John's shoulder. "Take your wife and children into the foyer," she suggested quietly. Gail swaddled a blanket around baby John and clutched him against her life-jacket. John swept pyjama-clad Kari into the air and struggled out of the lounge with eight-year-old Samantha's arms wrapped firmly around his legs. Outside, on the windswept promenade deck, John could sense, rather than see, the awesome power of the sea. The wind lashed his face with spume; it felt like the sting of a whip.

A steward eased baby John out of Gail's arms and helped her to half-crawl, half-walk through the mass of struggling bodies; she turned as John called, "Here, take Kari and Samantha." He thrust the children towards her.

A lifeboat was already dangling over the side, swinging wildly above the seething waves. Lorraine Betts, together with guitarist Moss Hills, and his magician friend Julian Butler, were forming the passengers into a straggling, staggering queue.

Captain Avranas was there, shepherding his wife and daughter into the lifeboat. He turned. "Lorraine, I must get help," he shouted, and then started to scramble into the tiny, already overcrowded boat. An arm reached out for his life-jacket and pulled him roughly back to the deck.

Baby John, then Kari and finally Samantha, were lifted into the lifeboat. Gail prepared to say goodbye to them, perhaps for ever. Please, God, look after them, she silently prayed. Lorraine slapped her on the shoulder. Gail looked around. "Go!" ordered Lorraine. With a sob of relief, Gail jumped into boat to join her children.

"Lower away!" Lorraine shouted. The boat fell into the night, lurching and crashing against the side of the ship before hitting the water with a spine-shattering thump. Mothers and children were tossed like rag dolls from their seats. Looking over the side from the promenade deck, Lorraine watched the boat swoop and corkscrew on the giant black waves. She heard the engine fire, crest a wave, and disappear into the blackness.

In the distance, plunging through the mountainous seas, she could see the lights of approaching ships. Rescue teams all along the coast, alerted by the rescue co-ordination centre in Cape Town, had swung into action.

In the lounge of the *Oceanos*, a crowd of young men was singing rugby songs. A solitary woman was crying, "I can't swim," she sobbed. Moss and Tracy Hills grabbed their guitars and jumped on to the stage. Soon everybody was singing.

Someone tapped John Adamson on the shoulder. "We need strong men to row the next lifeboat," said a voice in his ear. He crawled out of the lounge, no longer able to stand upright on the sloping, rolling deck, to where Lorraine Betts half-pushed him on to the waiting lifeboat. Looking back, he saw Captain Avranas struggling to reach the lifeboat, and someone pulling him away.

Slowly, painfully slowly, the passengers were shepherded in groups from the lounge to their lifeboat stations. Patiently, Lorraine Betts and Robin Boltman filled the boats before watching them slip away into the darkness. There were eight lifeboats on the *Oceanos*, enough for everybody on board. But only five had been got away.

"Help me count how many passengers are still in the lounge," Lorraine told her staff. They found there were still more than 250 people on board. In the dining room, just two decks down from the lounge, chairs were already floating as the sea began to sweep through the *Oceanos*.

"Move everybody up to the upper deck," she ordered. "When the ship starts to go down, we'll line up at the rails and jump into the sea. Meantime, someone must go up on the bridge to keep watch." It was 3am when the remaining passengers began to inch their way out of the lounge on to the open deck, clinging to each other for support, bruising themselves as the ship rolled and they were flung againt the bulkheads.

The bows of a black, rust-smeared ship loomed over the lifeboat in which Gail Adamson sat huddled with her children. A Panamanian tanker, *Great Nancy*, was the first of five rescue ships to reach the scene.

One by one, first the children and then their mothers were winched up to the ship's deck. Gail was led to the warmth of a cabin. On the bunk, carefully tucked in, the two girls were already sleeping peacefully. Baby John was kicking his legs and screaming blue murder.

Two hours later another lifeboat crashed alongside. Standing in the passage the women searched for the faces of their men folk. Dismayed, they watched as crewman after crewman, all from the *Oceanos*, pushed sheepishly past them, each one carrying baggage. There wasn't a single passenger among them. None of the women said a word, merely stared at the crewmen with contempt.

Hours later, the *Great Nancy* picked up a third boat. Joyously, Gail recognized her husband crowding with other survivors into the passage. She wrapped her arms around him. "The children are safe," she cried, tears pouring down her cheeks. John could not speak for relief.

When rescue helicopter pilot Chaz Goatley flew over the *Oceanos*, the ship's vast white hull was already wallowing ponderously, her rails awash, her stern beginning to lift clear of the water, her bows nose-diving into the sea. Hundreds of people, all in orange life-jackets, were lining the steeply heeling deck.

The helicopter hovered over the vessel, carrying two navy divers harnessed to a wire from the belly of the chopper. One, Paul Whiley, was dropped on to the stern and the other, Gary Scoular, was lowered into the bows. The passengers began to cheer.

Moss Hill slithered down the steeply sloping deck to greet diver Scoular. "I'm the ship's guitarist," he said.

"You can help me put people in the harness," said Scoular. "Where's the crew?"

Moss grimaced. "Gone in the boats."

"Nice one," said Scoular, bitterly.

In the stern section, Whiley shouted at a queue of passengers waiting to be rescued: "We'll hoist two people at a time." He could only just be heard over the constant howl of the wind and the clatter of helicopter rotor blades. "OK, who's first?"

Captain Avranas thrust his way past a line of young women, ignoring the tears running down their cheeks. He quickly buckled himself into one of the harnesses. Whiley gave the badges of rank on his shoulders a long, hard stare, then shrugged and let him go.

The line jerked and the captain became the first person to be air-lifted off the sinking deck of the *Oceanos*, open-mouthed passengers staring up at him in disbelief.

When the empty wire was returned from the chopper to the deck, the ship's radio officer was the next to force his way to the front of the queue, followed by the ship's purser and a deck-hand. Whiley hadn't time to argue with them. Seven people were carried on the first helicopter: the captain, two officers, a sailor, and three women. 243 people were still left on board.

One by one, with dawn breaking and the *Oceanos* all the time settling lower and lower into the water, the liner's passengers were winched to safety. But in the forward part of the ship, naval diver Gary Scoular detected a gradual but dramatic change in the way the vessel was lying in the water. He realized some way had to be found to speed up the evacuation.

He had spotted some tiny motor launches, used by passengers to potter around the smooth waters of their harbour stop-overs, stacked in the bow. He slithered down the steepening slope of the deck towards the very front of the ship.

Waves were crashing over the bows and loose oil drums were rolling across the deck. Then, as if by magic, a Filipino crewman mysteriously appeared at Scoular's side. Together they manhandled a launch into the sea. Scoular dived after it and hauled himself on board. The engine started first time. He yelled to Lorraine Betts and Julian Butler at the rail of the liner: "Bring people!"

One by one, passengers flung themselves into the sea and swam to the launch. A non-swimmer hesitated at the rail of the ship. Butler grabbed his life-jacket and dragged the man overboard with him. Scoular and Butler made six trips from the *Oceanos* to ships' lifeboats standing off from rescuing vessels. They saved about 40 people.

On the final trip Scoular shouted to Lorraine, "Come on!"

"Wait!" she yelled back, making her way to the bridge. She counted the heads of passengers still awaiting rescue. There were only a few, waiting patiently at the stern air-lift point. "Moss," she called, "I've been ordered off." Moss Hill gave a weary wave. Lorraine jumped into the sea. When she clawed her way over the side into the launch her watch had stopped at 10.20am.

From the window of the radio room on the bridge, Robin Boltman gave a thumbs up to Moss Hill. Moss was helping his wife Tracy push people up the deck to the air-lift point where two passengers, Piet Niemand and his grown-up son Peter, had taken over at the stern section harness. "Let go of the rails and raise your arms," Piet told people as they slipped the harness under their armpits and drew the buckles tight. Then he and his son gave a thumbs up: "Go!"

When only a handful of people were left on the stern, Piet urged his son to be winched to safety. The young man refused to leave. Piet reached down and gently helped an elderly woman, who had somehow been overlooked, to her feet. She could barely stand. "Son, take this lady up with you, as a favour to me."

It was a request Peter couldn't refuse. "Hold me as tight as you can," he smiled at the shivering woman. She wrapped her thin arms around him. Piet craned his neck so that he could watch his son and the frail burden clutched to him being winched to the safety of the helicopter.

Eventually, only Niemand, Whiley, Moss, Tracy and the mysterious Filipino seaman were left on the deck. The unidentified seaman, the only member of the liner's crew to stay with the ship until the end, read Psalm 23: "Yea, though I walk through the valley of the shadow of death, I will fear no evil; for thou art with me. . ."

Looking down from the bridge, Robin Boltman signed off over the radio: "*Oceanos* is about to go down. I'm leaving the bridge." He waved a salute down at Gary Scoular and Julian Butler who were standing off in the launch watching the ship go through her final death throes.

The naval diver Whiley and passenger Niemand were the last to be winched off the ship to a hovering helicopter.

The *Oceanos* toppled over and took her final plunge to the grave at 1.46pm, August 4, 1991. Every one of the 571 people on board were saved. That was the miracle of the *Oceanos*.

Lorraine Betts, Moss and Tracy Hill, Julian Butler, Robin Boltman and Piet Niemand were awarded the Wolraad medal, South Africa's highest award for civilian valour.

Helicopter pilot Chaz Goatley, and naval divers Gary Scoular and Paul Whiley were decorated by the South African Defence Force.

The Greek Maritime Board found Captain Yiannis Avranas and five of his senior officers guilty of negligence and of abandoning their passengers.

The Survivalist's Handbook

Chapter 3:

Finding Food

If you're in a survival situation for any length of time, you'll need to find food. Ideally, you'd need to eat meat and fish to keep your strength up, but you have to catch those first! Looking for plants, berries and roots is much easier but, remember, never eat anything you can't identify.

1. It sounds awful, but **stinging nettles** can be eaten – in fact you might have heard of nettle tea. Cover your hand for protection, and pick the tops of the plants. Boil them for ten minutes in a little water.

2. **Beech leaves** can be eaten raw, or boiled or steamed, but only pick the youngest and tenderest leaves. The youngest leaves of the **hawthorn** taste good raw – they have a nutty flavour.

3. **Dandelions** grow in all sorts of places. The young leaves, taken from the heart of the plant, are quite tasty raw or boiled for 20 minutes. Full-grown plants are too bitter to eat, but dandelion roots can be used as a vegetable.

4. You might find **watercress** growing in streams and ditches, but don't eat it raw

because it can carry disease. Cooked watercress isn't dangerous and even tastes quite nice.

5. **Berries** often look very tempting, but many are poisonous. Don't eat *any* berries unless you're absolutely sure what they are. And don't attempt to eat any **mushrooms** or fungus you find growing in the wild unless you really know what you're doing. Some mushrooms are safe to eat but others are extremely dangerous, and it's often difficult to tell the difference.

6. You'll often find **seaweed** on the menu in a Japanese restaurant. It can be quite a delicacy and is actually very nourishing, especially the 'laver' variety. It's a slow process, though. You'll need to wash the seaweed thoroughly and boil it for four hours! When the laver sheets break up into tiny pieces it is ready to eat, and can be made into a paste.

7. You can even tap **trees** for their sap. The birch, beech, sycamore, hickory and especially the maple are all good sources. Sap is a great energy source because it has a high sugar content, but remember that trees are protected by law, so this is only an emergency measure.

8. **Honey** from wild bees is so full of energy that it will restore the energy of the

most exhausted survialist, but watch out for those bees!

9.   Eating **slugs** and **insects** might sound horrible, but it could save your life in an emergency. Snails, worms and slugs can be eaten, but avoid sea snails and any snail that is brightly coloured. The legs of grasshoppers can also be eaten, and so can beetle grubs, caterpillars, butterflies and moths. Find out how to identify a few different kinds of edible grubs or bugs, and eat only the ones you know are definitely safe. Never eat anything unless you are absolutely sure what it is – some insects, like yellow ladybirds and certain types of ants and moths, are poisonous.

10.   You should always take food along with you if you're going to be out in the wild for any length of time. Dried fruits and nuts are easy to carry, and a good source of fibre and protein. Sweets aren't very nourishing, but provide lots of energy. Freeze-dried meals are also available in many shops. They're convenient and don't weigh very much, but need to be soaked in some of your valuable water before you eat them. Salt and sugar are both good flavourings, and of course salt is essential for life.

Skydive

P arachute accidents are few and far between. "It may seem dangerous but it is really one of the safest sports," says skydiving veteran Ronnie O'Brien.

So in April 1991, it was sheer coincidence that Ronnie, nearly two thousand metres up in the skies above Cambridgeshire, England, had just 30 seconds to save two sport-para jumpers from crashing to the earth, while six hundred miles away in Italy, at almost precisely the same time of day, the captain of Britain's paragliding team was plummeting towards what looked like certain death.

Even the weather was similar. "The perfect day for skydiving," recalls Ronnie. At 7.30am he was standing on the grass of Sibson Airfield. Far above him, puff-ball clouds in a cobweb-blue sky heralded a beautiful day.

In Italy, 23-year-old Jocky Sanderson, captain of a nine-strong British team, stood on the slopes of Monte Caina, 40 miles north-west of Venice. It was the final morning of the year's first international paragliding contest and Jocky was preparing for take-off.

So was first-time para jumper Richard Maynard, back at the Sibson Airfield in England. Richard was a computer analyst from London. He was about to climb into a Skyvan transport plane before leaping into the unknown, strapped in tandem to an experienced instructor, Mike Smith, from Peterborough Parachute Centre.

"Tandem skydiving is a chance to discover the thrill of high altitude free-fall without having to learn the skills," Richard had been assured.

"Seems all right to me. Let's go," said Richard.

"I'm terrified," said another tandem novice due to make his first jump on the same day.

"They say it's the world's greatest high," Richard grinned.

Ronnie O'Brien was to skydive with them and film Richard's rooky jump with a video and stills camera attached to his helmet.

At 3,000 metres Mike Smith tapped Richard on the shoulder and they shuffled towards the aircraft's rear cargo exit "like a pantomine horse in a three-legged race". Both men were buckled at the waist into a dual parachute harness. A reserve chute, strapped to Mike's chest, was pressed hard against Richard's back.

"Face up! Face up!" shouted Mike from the edge of the exit, reaching over Richard's shoulder to force his chin up so that their tandem-bodies would be arched as they left the aircraft, ensuring they would float face-to-earth in the classic free-fall position.

The plane climbed to 3,600 metres. Over the sill of the exit door, they saw the flat farmlands of Cambridgeshire far beneath them, veiled by a haze of blue mist.

"Exit position!" yelled Mike in Richard's ear. "Ready...!" At "Set...!" Ronnie O'Brien pushed himself backwards out of the plane, ready to get camera shots of their tandem exit.

"Go!"

All Richard can clearly remember about the first moments after being jostled out of the aircraft by his tandem partner was a feeling that he had left his stomach behind, as they dropped nearly one kilometre in the first 15 seconds, and, at the same time, an overwhelming sense of exhilaration as they hurtled through space at a speed accelerating up to 180 mph (290 kph) – about as fast as Formula One racing drivers roar down the straights at

Monza and Silverstone. "With the aircraft gone," he said, "the only sound was the wind."

As the pair continued to fall, all the time dropping faster and faster, Ronnie O'Brien captured them on film. Soon, because he was skydiving solo and was lighter than the tandem pair, Ronnie was left 90 metres above them. He was to have a bird's eye view of all that followed – like watching somebody else's nightmare.

He saw Mike Smith pull the cord to release a small drogue parachute which would slow the pair to 120 mph (190 kph), the speed at which solo skydivers are comfortably able to control their direction of glide. The drogue is attached to a 4.5 metre line called a bridle cord attached to the base of the instructor's main parachute container on his back. Once inflated, the tandem pair could skydive down to almost 2,000 metres where Mike Smith would pull a rip-cord to detach the bridle cord and automatically open their main parachute.

But things began to go alarmingly wrong.

Instead of deploying properly, the drogue began flapping, wrapping the bridle-cord around the tandem pair like string tightening around a parcel. Richard tried to force it away with his arm but the action caused the two men to roll over, trapping Mike's neck as if it was in a hangman's noose.

The pair, no longer suspended horizontally, were now spinning violently, still plummeting towards the earth. They were down to just under 3,000 metres.

Mike Smith reached for the emergency knife in the thigh pocket of his jump suit so that he could cut the bridle cord of the drogue and release its ever-tightening strangle hold on his neck. Then, even though the pair would be deprived of a main parachute, he could deploy their reserve and they would float safely down to earth. But he never got to the knife. At 2,300 metres he blacked out.

Astonishingly, Mike's tandem partner Richard was blissfully unaware that anything was wrong. "I thought being buffeted about was all part of the show. I even suspected they were playing a practical joke on me, to see how much I could take."

High above, his arms outstretched like wings to slow his decent, Ronnie O'Brien looked down. He quickly realized that something had gone badly wrong. But he wasn't dismayed. At any moment he expected to see the 37-square-metre reserve parachute flutter out and take charge of the spiralling, plummeting tandem pair. He waited in vain. The next moment he clamped his arms flush to his sides and nose-dived like a falcon towards the stricken tandem.

"I had only once chance to get it right," he said afterwards. "If I misjudged my angle of descent I would hurtle straight past the pair and they would be as good as dead."

He made no mistake. At 2,100 metres he was in front of the pair, gesturing wildly at the reserve parachute handle on his own chest, prompting Mike Smith to pull his own.

Through his goggles, the pendulum-swinging Richard saw Ronnie waving to them. He grinned.

Again Ronnie pointed frantically towards the reserve chute handle. It was then that he saw Mike's neck was trapped in the bridle cord.

I'll have to try to pull his reserve handle myself, thought Ronnie. There's no other way to save them.

But how? The pair were swinging so wildly that one

moment they were a metre or so away from Ronnie's outstretched arms, the next maybe twelve. There were no more than 30 seconds left before the tandem pair would crash into the earth.

He lunged. And missed!

"It was a disaster," Ronnie recalled later. "I had now slipped well below them. We were now at 1,500 metres." Mike and Richard were no more than 25 seconds from death.

Ronnie spreadeagled his arms and legs in order to brake his speed. The tandem pair slowly fell towards him. Eventually he was just above their swinging bodies. He dived, fell on top of them and frantically wrapped his arms around them.

Nine hundred metres and 15 seconds from impact, Ronnie's fingers feverishly searched for Mike's reserve chute handle. He found it! He pulled. It slipped from his hand!

Twelve seconds from impact . . . 760 metres above the ground . . . Ronnie's scrabbling hand found the reserve handle again. He tugged.

That's it, that's it . . .!

The reserve parachute opened and the tandem pair were jerked up and away from him. He pulled the handle of his own chute, heard it give the soft, explosive crack of a parachute deploying, and looked up. Now, high over his head, above the quilted plumpness of his own canopy, Ronnie could see the fully deployed parachute of the tandem pair. He was sweating. He took a deep breath and yelled:

"Yesssss!"

*　　*　　*

In Italy, Jocky Sanderson was high on adrenalin, his nerve-ends tingling with excitement. He was already Britain's top paraglider. Today, in the international contest, was his chance to prove himself the best in the world. He stood poised to take off, 1,000 metres up, from the grassy slopes of northern Italy's Monte Caina.

"It was a paraglider's paradise," he remembered, "a brilliant day for flying, in a region of abundant thermals, or up-draughts of warm air, essential for staying aloft."

There is a big difference between free-fall parachuting and paragliding. Skydivers leap from aeroplanes to perform complicated aerial acrobatics before their parachutes open. Paragliders, taking off from high places, seek out thermal up-draughts – those currents of warm air which rise from the earth the way a draught of heat rises from sun-warmed stones – on which they can soar upwards in order to make long cross-country flights.

Jocky fiddled with the straps of his helmet, and then looked round, checking again that the cords running from the four straps of his body harness to the white paraglider – a 27-square-metre wing of lightweight nylon spread out flat – lay untangled on the grass behind him. Next to him, and above him, the slope was a kaleidoscope of colours where other canopies, like giant bed-sheets drying in the early morning sun, were draped on the ground behind their owners' backs. Soon, the sky would fill with reds and oranges and yellows and pinks and whites as 150 competitors took off in search of the thermals which would help them along the 50-kilometre course.

On the ground, Jocky was a devil-may-care character, always ready for a joke and a laugh. In the air, and immediately before a flight, he was single-minded with concentration. He left nothing to chance.

Over his shoulder he ran an expert eye along the length and width of his collapsed paraglider: two rectangular sheets of lightweight fabric sewn together into 50 tubes of nylon, or "cells", open along the leading edge and extending across the width of the canopy. Each seam had been meticulously checked, the dozens of lines from harness to canopy had been painstakingly inspected, and the control loops on the 45-centimetre-long wire straps attached to his body harness had been renewed.

"There goes a dummy," someone shouted. Jocky looked up. The "wind dummy" balloons which had been sent up by race marshalls ever since day break to test the strength of the air thermals had, one by one, failed to rise into the air. Now, though, one had suddenly soared upwards like a bird.

At last, the thermals are creating lift, thought Jockey. It's time to go. The other pilots reached the same decision. Together they sprinted down the slope, their paragliders trailing behind them like kites being towed into the air. Jocky's boots pounded over the grass. Suddenly, as if by magic, he was plucked from the ground as the boiling up-current of a thermal whisked his paraglider wing into the sky. Jocky Sanderson was airborne. Around him other pilots jostled for airspace as a turmoil of air currents sent them soaring upwards in a mêlée of bodies and canopies.

With the skill of four years' paragliding experience, Jocky pulled on one of the control loops so that his canopy would swoop away from the other competitors. From the corner of his eye he saw two pilots pull their reserve parachutes and retire from the contest when their canopies ran into a freak air pocket and collapsed.

He manoeuvred his canopy this way and that, seeking out one thermal after another, soaring higher and higher.

At take-off plus 70 minutes he had left the pack behind him. The variometer, or pressure gauge, strapped to his left thigh showed that he was 760 metres above the valley floor, almost touching the clouds. Jocky was ecstatic; he knew he was among the leaders.

Ten minutes later disaster struck. The variometer began to click in alarm. Without warning he had begun to fall at 250 metres a minute!

That's fast, he muttered grimly to himself.

Suddenly, the left hand side of his canopy collapsed like the broken wing of a bird. Jocky began to fall out of the sky at an even faster rate than before!

He still wasn't dismayed though. He knew exactly what to do; pull down on his right-hand control line while pumping the left-hand line to reinflate the canopy's cells. At the same time, he shifted his body weight away from the collapsed half of the wing. Nothing happened!

The variometer began clicking even more frantically. He glanced down. Now he was falling at about 450 metres a minute. Beneath his feet, getting closer by the second, was a boulder-strewn gorge. He took a quick look upwards. Well over three-quarters of the canopy wing had collapsed. He had never known anything like this to happen before. Slowly at first, then faster and faster, he felt himself corkscrewing round and round like a weight on a piece of tightly twisted elastic. He pumped even harder at the control lines. Nothing, no response.

Reaching down, he felt for the rip-cord which would open his reserve chute. He was falling out of the sky so fast that he was now only 150 metres from the ground. If he was going to deploy his reserve chute it had to be now or never. But he hesitated. Something told him to wait. There was a faint response on the right control cord.

"Fly, baby, fly!" shouted Jocky aloud.

But the paraglider continued its headlong plunge towards the ground. Rocks in the gorge were stabbing up at him like the points of spears. In a blur the tops of trees at the side of the gorge flashed beneath his feet. His boots crashed through them, splintering them like matchwood. He tucked up his knees, bracing himself, waiting to plummet to the floor of the gorge.

The bone-crushing impact never came. Unbelievably, the canopy gained some lift. Briefly, he was floating! Then, to his dismay, he sensed that the canopy had collapsed again. Grim faced, he tugged furiously at the control loops, his arms working like pistons. Still, he found himself being hurtled towards the floor of the gorge.

"Open, damn you!" he swore.

The canopy jerked once. Then again. The cords from his harness to the canopy snapped taut. He was flying again! He glanced down at his variometer. Just 45 metres from the ground! He had fallen for almost a kilometre, the final 300 metres in just 40 seconds.

Jocky soared out of the shadow of the gorge into the sun. A thermal shot him up to 180 metres. Beneath him two hikers were staring up, open-mouthed.

Jocky worked his way out of the gorge and landed safely in a meadow just over six kilometres short of the contest's finish at Bassano del Grappa. Because of his early landing he was placed fifty-eighth. The British team came sixth.

After his close brush with death, has he been put off paragliding for ever? Not a bit of it.

"What happened was a freak accident," he insists. "I love the sport – it's the most joyous and exhilarating experience I know."

The
Survivalist's
Handbook

Chapter 4:

Finding
Your
Way

Have you ever wondered how you could find your way in the wilderness without a map or compass? It's possible, and people have been doing it successfully for centuries. Some of the techniques used for navigation are very sophisticated, but there are some simple ones that you could try for yourself, using a compass to check your results.

1. If you have a compass but no watch you can still work out the time. When the sun is at its highest point in the sky it is exactly north of you (in the northern hemisphere) or south of you (in the southern hemisphere). The sun reaches its highest point at 12 noon, so when it is directly north of you then you know it is 12 noon. You can use this principle to tell the approximate time of day, whatever the position of the sun.

2. You can find out which way is north using the sun and a stick! Put your stick upright in the ground, and towards midday start measuring the shadow the stick casts by putting a stone at the end of the shadow. Do this every fifteen minutes or so. The shadow will gradually shorten towards noon and lengthen from then on, so the shortest

shadow will be cast at noon. The shortest shadow will therefore point north in the northern hemisphere and south in the southern hemisphere.

3.   A needle, a bowl of water and a blade of grass can be used as a compass! Magnetize the needle, using a magnet or by brushing it against silk. Float a blade of grass in a bowl of water, then put the needle on top of the grass. It should point in a north-south direction.

4.   The stars are a good way of finding direction. In the northern hemisphere, the easiest way to find north is to look for the Plough, which is also called the Great Bear or Big Dipper. Actually, it looks more like a saucepan with a bent handle – look in a book on star constellations and find a picture of it. The two stars which make up the side of the saucepan opposite the handle point towards the North Star (also called the Pole Star), which shows the exact position of the North Pole. In the southern hemisphere you need to look for the Southern Cross. The two stars that make up the longest axis of the cross point south – not exactly, but near enough to go by.

5.   Most people know that you can tell the age of a tree by the rings in the tree stump, but it's a little known fact that the rings will

be wider apart on the north (in the northern hemisphere) or south (in the southern hemisphere).

6. Trees and shrubs standing on their own are affected by wind and sun. So if you know which way the prevailing winds blow in the area you are in, for example south-west, the wind will have swept the branches of single trees and shrubs towards the north-east. More moss will grow on the side of the tree trunk which receives the least sunlight.

7. Other plants and animals make good direction indicators. If you're in southern Africa, you can find north using the North Pole plant, which is named after the direction it leans towards. The African weaver bird only ever builds its nest on the west side of trees.

8. Did you know that there are actually three "norths"? True north is the position of the earth's geographical North Pole, magnetic north is the direction your compass points, and grid north is the north marked on maps. In most parts of the world, these three points are similar enough to make very little difference. But there are some places where the three are quite different. This is called "magnetic variation" and is marked on most maps, so that anyone travelling in that area can adjust their compass reading accordingly.

Lost
at Sea

Australian Michelle Hamilton was 21 years old, adventurous, athletic and intelligent. When she first arrived on the tiny Philippine island of Baracay, for a holiday with her mother, she fell in love with it. The island was a perfect holiday retreat – ivory-white beaches fringed by palm trees which cast shimmering reflections on a turquoise-blue sea.

Ahh, another perfect day in paradise, thought Michelle on the morning of March 9, 1989. Always ready for a challenge, ever eager to pit her skills against the elements, she had borrowed a miniature outrigger-canoe in which she could paddle all the way round the tiny island. She dressed in a striped bikini, and for clambering ashore on the other side of the island she slipped on her black trainers. In a string bag she packed tapes and a cassette player, a camera, something to read, snorkel, flippers and a mask.

Her first objective was the southernmost tip of the island. She put on her headphones, turned the volume up high, and began a strenuous session of paddling. In the crystal-clear water beneath her canoe, a school of blue and yellow fish darted in and out of the multi-coloured coral. From the corner of her eye, less than 100 metres away, were splashes of vivid colour where holiday makers sunbathed on the beach.

She again focussed her eyes on the tip of the island. It didn't appear to be getting any closer. In fact, the canoe seemed to have drifted away from the shore.

This is proving more difficult than I thought, she mused. But what the heck, I wanted a challenge.

She paddled on. A local fishing boat, her decks crowded with waving fishermen, passed close by. She couldn't

understand why the men stared at her so hard, so
questioningly. But she had become so concerned with
the canoe's steady drift away from the island that she
needed to concentrate all her mind and energy on
paddling. Grimly, she worked the canoe's bows round
so it was heading directly for the beach. It was 1pm.
There would still be time for lunch at the popular floating
bar.

With a rising sense of dismay she gradually came to
realize that the beach was not getting any closer. In fact, it
was slowly slipping further and further away.

What on earth is happening? Why am I not getting any
closer? she thought, and her heart began to beat faster as
she realized that the canoe was being swept out to sea by
an ocean current. She wanted to shout for help, but the
beach was now a kilometre away and her cries would not
have been heard. She ripped off her headphones and began
paddling in a surge of panic.

The sea was no longer mirror-smooth. A rising wind
had whipped the waves into a chop. Beneath the surface
she saw the shadowy wings of a giant manta ray. A huge
rainbow-speckled fish closed its gaping jaws on a shoal of
neons before sinking into the awesome blackness of the
deep. She began to think of the man-eating sharks which
preyed in the waters off the Philippines.

Please God, she thought, don't let a wave toss me into
the sea.

Her feverish grip on the rough wooden paddle had
shredded her hands raw. It was now 4.30pm. She had been
fighting the ocean current for five and a half hours. Her
arms felt like lead weights.

How have I let this happen? she wanted to scream. It

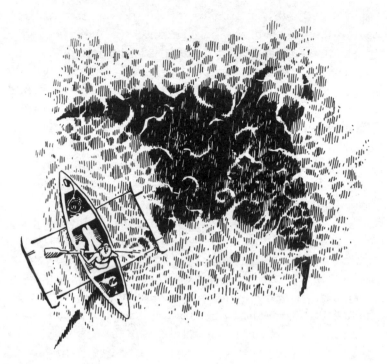

would be dark in another hour and a half. *What am I going to do?*

Fearfully, she weighed her options. *I could swim for it. I know I'm tired, but I'm fit. The beach is no more than half-a-mile away, if that; I can make it before nightfall. When I get tired I'll float on my back.*

But as she looked into the dark hollows of the foreboding waves, her skin crawled at the thought of lowering herself into the water where every shadow looked like the lurking form of a predatory monster.

She began putting on her snorkelling equipment. She

scanned the ocean. *Where is everybody? I can't believe no one is looking for me.* She gave a howl of anguish and despair, took a deep breath and prepared to jump over the side.

"Don't leave the boat!" a loud voice commanded.

Rescue! I've been saved! Michelle swung round. "Help! Help!" she called out. "Who's there? Where are you?" But there was no one; Michelle had imagined the voice.

She slumped into the bottom of the canoe. The voice had rendered her powerless, unable to do anything but huddle in the bilge as day slowly turned to night. On the other evenings of that holiday she had basked in the beauty of the tropical sunset; now she would have done anything to keep the sun from plunging over the horizon.

Suddenly it was dark; in no time at all, the sun touched the surface of the ocean and disappeared, the way it does in the tropics. A thick layer of cloud veiled the moon. A storm was gathering.

When the first spooks of darkness began to sap Michelle's reserves, she wanted to 'pull the covers over her head'. It was a classic sign of distress. As she put it: "I felt like an abandoned child about to be washed over the edge of the world." She curled up in the bottom of the boat, her hips wedged between the sides, and tried to ignore the terrors of the night.

But there was to be no escape. Already, the wind had turned the sea into a turmoil of angry waves. The fragile canoe began to plunge and soar on a seething turbulence of white water. Waves washed into the boat, filling it dangerously. Michelle began bailing for her life.

Thunder claps exploded overhead, sheets of rain speared on to Michelle's naked back. A flash of lightning illuminated everything: the tossing, water-filled canoe, the ranks of gigantic waves which were sweeping down upon it. The canoe crawled up each roller-coaster wave, teetered on the crest, then swooped down the other side, tossed this way and that like a helpless piece of cork. Michelle's knuckles were white where they clung to the sides of the boat. Sheets of sea water crashed over her. Her eyes were blinded by salt.

A flurry of thoughts raced through her brain. *What will I do if I capsize? Will I be able to swim to the canoe in the darkness? Will I even be able to find it? And if I do, will I be able to cling to it? Will I have the strength to hang on? Am I going to die?*

Her nightmare, the nightmare of her first night at sea, was washed away with the first signs of dawn. Relief swept over her as her eyes strained for a sight of land. Surely, she thought, with more than 7,000 islands in the Philippines' group, I will eventually drift to land? Yet there was nothing, just rank upon rank of towering waves, racing towards the canoe. One, bigger than the rest, plucked the boat from the surface of the sea and threw it violently into the air. Michelle found herself falling through space. The boat had gone. She found herself sucked into a suffocating welter of foam, swallowed by the ocean. This is it, Michelle, she thought, as dizziness overtook her. Finally, she found herself back on the surface, greedily sucking great gulps of air. Again, she felt a gigantic undertow grasp hold of her body, turning her over and over, swirling her round and round, thrusting her deep beneath the surface. Again, she resurfaced, spluttering, gasping, retching on sea water.

The boat has gone! Terror gripped her. *No, no, there it is. Thank God! Thank God!* The tremendous relief she felt when she swam to the boat was short-lived. It had capsized, jettisoning the contents of her string bag into the sea. Helpless, she watched her possessions sink beneath her. Something spurred her to make a wild grab for her flippers, before scrambling on to the overturned boat and wrapping her arms in a vicelike grip round the hull.

Battered by the waves, it took her half an hour to put the flippers on and plunge beneath the boat, grabbing it from underneath and straining with all her strength to right it. It wouldn't budge. It was as though it was bolted to the sea. She tried again. Still it wouldn't move. Wearily, she dragged herself back on to the hull, only to find herself slipping uncontrollably back into the water. She tried again. A slimy film of green algae made it impossible to cling to the bottom of the boat. Gripping on to the outrigger, she felt a mountainous deluge of water smash against her back, wrenching her away from the boat, spinning her down, down into the sea.

Oh stop! she wanted to scream. *Give me a break. I can't stand any more. I have no strength to fight.*

Somehow, she struggled back to the surface and splashed towards the boat. By scissoring her legs over the outrigger bar she was able to cling on, despite the waves which continued to crash over her. The morning sun began to warm her tortured body. She felt hope and strength returning.

I'm alive! I'm alive, she sobbed with relief. With the dawning of new hope she renewed her struggle for survival. Come on Michelle, you can't just wallow in self-pity, she told herself. Gradually, the storm passed away. Weakly, she began paddling with her flippers. She kept that up for an hour until her legs were seized by burning cramps.

Slowly, painfully slowly, the day passed without sight of another vessel, without a sign of land. As the sun plunged into the ocean, Michelle stared into the approaching darkness and prayed: "If you're listening to me, I'm not afraid of death itself, more the uncertainty of not knowing. God, am I going to die?"

Michelle is convinced God spoke back to her. A voice which seemed to shatter the night air said, "No, you are not going to die."

"At that moment," says Michelle, "my belief in God was affirmed."

With ten hours of darkness before her, and the wind howling eerily across the surface of the ocean, she clung to the upturned hull. She desperately wanted to stretch out and go to sleep. But she told herself she must stay awake if she was to live. She began to shiver uncontrollably. Reluctantly, knowing that the only way to escape the bitter wind was to submerge herself in the water, she slipped into the sea. She was still so cold that her whole body felt numb; soon, she could feel nothing. Against her will she began to think of sharks – she knew she was easy prey. She tried to dispel the thought, but failed. During the night one of the canoe's outriggers was wrenched from the hull by the waves. Every time other waves crashed against the remaining outrigger it creaked and groaned; if that one, too, was to break away from the boat there would be no way for Michelle to retain her grip on the algae-covered hull.

Slowly, night turned to day. As she watched the sun crawling out of the sea, the boat swooped up on to the crest of a wave. Far off, perhaps 15 miles away, were the three peaks of islands! And the boat was drifting towards them! They were the most beautiful sight Michelle had ever seen.

"Oh thank you, thank you," she called out.

She calculated it would take about 12 hours before the current carried her to the islands. It would be dark again by then. She began paddling furiously, astounded that her weakened body still had reserves of strength.

A wave lifted the boat high in the air, enabling her to see the islands more clearly. They were covered in dense forest.

Will I survive on a deserted island? she wondered. Full of renewed optimism she began to make plans.

I must try to get there before nightfall. Then I will find shelter and pull the boat high up the beach. I mustn't take chances. Trying to work some saliva into her parched mouth, she moved her cracked lips. Her tongue was swollen. Her every pore craved fresh water. *I must find water. But I mustn't eat unfamiliar plants and fruits. They might make me ill. I'd rather go hungry.*

She wondered if the islands were inhabited. *Headhunters!* This was quite conceivable, especially in the Phillipines where there were, and still are, blood-thirsty pirates waiting to prey on passing vessels and their crews.

Then something made her look round into the ocean behind her. At first she thought it was an apparition. But no. The fins of two sharks were slicing through the surface towards her!

She hauled herself on to the boat's slimy hull, not daring to take her eyes off the approaching sharks. In her mind, she had relived the same nightmare scenario over and over again during the past three days . . . sharks slowly circling the canoe, nudging it with their hideous snouts, tipping her into the water, their razor sharp teeth sinking into her flesh . . .

As her fear-stricken eyes watched the fins continue to cut a path through the water, a wave swept her into the sea. She resurfaced, ready to splash out for the boat. But something stopped her, an inborn awareness that sharks consider splashing a signal that prey is close by. Deliberately, and slowly, she swam for the upturned hull, not daring to look behind to see if the sharks were following. Careful not to make even a ripple she reached the boat and hauled herself up, searching frantically for the fins. They were swimming away into the distance.

Her heart had only just regained its normal beat when there was a low, rumbling noise behind her. She swivelled round and froze. Powering towards her, 500 metres away, was a ship. There was no sign of life on board. A wave crashed over Michelle, tossing her into the sea. Frantically, she swam back to the boat, staring up at the ship's massive side as it roared past her. There was still no sign of anyone on deck. She tried to scream, but only managed a hoarse croak. She could see the stern as the ship moved away. Still, there was nobody on deck. Then, figures appeared. One pointed in her direction. The ship finally halted about two kilometres away, the crew beckoning for Michelle to swim to them.

Reluctantly, not knowing if she had the strength to swim that far, she slipped into the water. Wearily, she struck out for the ship. It took her some 30 excruciating minutes to swim to within a metre or so of the ship's side. She was totally spent and in agony. Brown faces were staring down at her in amazement. They threw a rope down the steep side. It swung to and fro like a pendulum.

With a despairing sob Michelle lunged for it and clung on. A wave smashed her against the ship; skin was ripped from her shoulder as if she had been slashed by claws.

"Hold on tight," one of the men called out in English. "We'll pull you up."

With every jot of her remaining strength Michelle clung to the rope, her arms tearing from their sockets as her rescuers hauled her up the side, her sunburned stomach and legs ripping on the rusty metal. The pain was so intense she almost let go. Suddenly hands reached down for her outstretched arms. The touch of a human hand made her want to cry with joy as she was hauled on to the deck.

Oh, thank you, God. I've made it. Michelle was saved.

"Americano mermaid," she heard one of her rescuers say as she slipped into unconsciousness.

The ship that saved Michelle was *F.V.Alyss*, a Philippines fishing vessel. The crew tenderly cared for her tortured body as they whisked her to Manila at top speed, plying her with orange juice and tiny portions of sliced mangoes. She was as red as a boiled lobster. All of her body, except the tiny areas covered by her bikini, was covered in terrible burns caused by the sun, her skin was wrinkled like the skin of an 80-year-old, the glands in her throat were so swollen they jutted out like golf balls and her lips looked as though they had been blown up by a bicycle pump.

As the sea-water began to evaporate from her skin, the severity of her dehydration and burns became apparent. Salt was ingrained into every pore, making her skin feel as stiff as cardboard. She felt as though she was sitting on top of a fire.

"But I was alive," recalls Michelle, happily. Back on dry land she found herself wanting to shake people, to tell them to make the most of their precious gift of life.

"I would never again take for granted each morning sunrise. I would never forget that every breath I took was a gift from God," she says.

The Survivalist's Handbook

Chapter 5:

Fishing for Food and Cooking

Fish are a good food source, and could be the *only* source of food in some survival situations. There are many more ways to catch fish than with a fishing rod and line. Did you know fish can be tickled, groped, snared, babbed for or lured? And once you've managed to catch your fish, there are various ways of cooking it.

1. Many different types of fresh and sea water fish can be safely eaten, but it's wise to make sure you recognize the type of fish you have caught and know for certain that it's safe to eat. Shark's liver, for example, is poisonous. And watch out for the many different kinds of fish that can hurt you.

2. "Tickling" is the art of "hypnotizing" a trout before plucking it from the water! Experienced ticklers lower their hands into the water very gently, and slowly brush their "tickling" fingers along the belly of the fish; then they grasp the trout firmly and fling it on to the bank.

3. "Groping" simply means whisking a fish out of the water and into a container by hand, and is usually done in a shallow stream or low-tide rock pools. However, it's far from easy to become a successful groper!

4.   Pike and salmon can be snared with a wire snare, shaped like a noose and attached to the end of the pole. Both fish tend to hang motionless in the water, so that a skilful snarer can work the snare over the fish's body, finally pulling it tight to catch the fish.

5.   "Babbing" is an efficient method of catching eels. You'll need some worms, some strong cord and some wool. The wool is tied around a dozen or so worms and attached to the cord. When an eel bites the worms, its teeth become entangled in the wool.

6.   There are various kinds of traps for fish, and the simplest is a tidal rock pool. The pool should be baited with, for example, crushed shellfish, so that fish will be attracted by the bait and become trapped in the pool when the tide goes out.

7.   Hooks can be made out of safety-pins or a piece of strong wire, or even from the thorns of a bramble bush. You could attach your homemade hook to a fishing line made from the strong, fibrous stems of a nettle!

8.   Once you've caught your fish and killed it, it's important that you eat it as soon as possible. Fish go bad very quickly unless they're preserved in some way.

9.   Did you know that you can boil water or

cook food without pots or pans? A shallow hole in the ground, lined with a ground sheet, makes a good basin. Fill it with water and drop in some stones that have been heated in a fire until they are red hot (using sticks to pick them up), and you can cook food in the boiling water. Keep the water boiling by removing stones from the water as they cool and replacing them with hot ones.

10.   Food can be grilled on a flat stone that has been heated in a fire until it's red hot. The stone will retain the heat from the fire for long enough to cook the food.

11.   You can bake food by wrapping it in clay or damp paper, then burying it in the hot ashes of a fire which has been burning for a few hours. Food can be left to cook for six to eight hours, providing the fire is not built up, without getting burnt.

12.   You can even improvise your own oven, either by lining a hole with stones or by building a three-sided oven from stones and putting a flat stone over the top. Light a fire inside your oven, then when the stones are really hot, the fire can be raked out and food placed inside.

Hopefully you wouldn't be alone in an emergency situation. Always ask an adult to help you: fires can easily get out of hand.

Alone in the Ice

Finished my last pipe of baccy today. There is now precious little left to live for. Can have light only for meals which consist of porridge just warmed up, biscuit, cold pemmican[1] and marge. This means that the house[2] has got very cold and is covered with hoar frost up to the roof. Still impossible to get outside. Feet keep freezing up and have to be always taking off socks and warming them in my hands. Hardly any paraffin left or candles. I suppose I shall soon be reduced to chewing snow. At present am reduced to a pint of water a day and under a pound of food . . . What wouldn't I give to be . . . eating a beef and onion pudding!

Things looked black. He was alone, just as he had been for 128 days, alone in the ice where temperatures constantly fell 60 degrees below freezing. His food had run out, he no longer had enough fuel for lighting or heating or melting snow for water. He lived every minute of every day in almost total darkness. Yet, astonishingly, he was to survive for a total of 151 days.

One newspaper of the time hailed 26-year-old Augustine Courtauld's survival as: 'A triumph of human endurance.' He was fêted by the press and the public wherever he went. His feat of surviving alone in the wastes of the Arctic, with only a little food, for over 150 days, made his adventure as famous as that of Sir Robert Falcon Scott

1 Originally made by North American Indians, pemmican consists of lean meat which is dried, pounded, and mixed with melted fat to form a paste, then pressed into cakes. It was once favoured by explorers as a convenient means of carrying preserved food with minimum bulk.
2 The house was a tent buried beneath twelve feet of frozen snow.

who had lost his life in a race for the South Pole some 20 years earlier.

Yet, strangely, Augustine Courtauld's battle for survival has been all but forgotten.

Ever since he was a boy, Augustine had been intrigued by those vast regions of the world which, in the early years of the twentieth century, were still largely unexplored. Thanks to wealthy and indulgent parents he had trekked to the unmapped mountains of Greenland, he had travelled with Tuareg nomads through the Sahara, and he had single-handedly sailed his home-made boat wherever the whim would take him.

Now, after finding a bowler-hatted city job 'irksome', he had joined the 1930/31 British Arctic Expedition to explore the snowy wastes of Greenland. The expedition's official objective was to travel overland across the ice cap of Greenland and set up a meteorological station on the spine of the ice cap itself. Unofficially, the fourteen-man expedition, with an average age of 25, intended to seek adventure.

The meteorological station was successfully set up and running 240 kilometres northwest of the base camp at Angmagssalik Bay by 2 October 1930. Two men were left to man the station until a relief party arrived early in November. They were, in fact, relieved one month later than expected.

Augustine Courtauld was a member of the six-man team originally sent out to relieve the met station. In fifteen days the team managed to travel just 24km, fighting every inch of the way against bitter, howling Arctic gales and blizzards. On some days they were able to do nothing but huddle inside their tents, listening to the wind. On others, it sometimes took them six hours to dig out of the wind-blasted snow before they were able to pack the sledges and be on their way. Throughout the journey, and during his subsequent five-month ordeal, Courtauld kept a diary:

5 November: Snow drifted right up over the tent entrance, so causing the two walls to come together and make the tent very cold. Got out about 3pm to feed the dogs. Wind furious. Could only walk against it with face turned away. Most of the dogs were buried in the snow with only their noses out. Some of them did not seem to want their pemmican. Inside of tent covered with hoar frost, which drips on to us. We are now on half-rations which, fortunately, are large enough to keep us going.

Their lack of progress, and the speed with which their meagre rations were being consumed, caused increasing concern. Three sledges and three men were sent back to base. Freddie Chapman, Lawrence Wager and Courtauld struggled on towards the met station on their own. But their biggest problem remained: by the time the remaining three sledges reached their destination there would not be sufficient supplies for two men to be left at the station when the others departed back to base. Courtauld volunteered to be left alone at the ice cap station – if they ever succeeded in reaching it.

Conditions had deteriorated still further by 15 November. Temperatures wavered between –20° and –32°F. All three men were in constant pain from frost-bite. Even inside their tents they were never warm, chilled to the marrow by hoar frost. Whenever the wind subsided enough for them to dig their way out of their tents, they discovered that the dogs had chewed their own traces through hunger. And when they were eventually on the move, the sledges kept overturning on "knife-edge drifts as hard as concrete".

15 November: Drifts very bad, sledges overturned every few yards. Freddie's sledge showed signs of breaking up, so we camped. Decided to lighten his sledge and only take on enough food for one man (self) at ice cap. We shall therefore only take 4 instead.

21 November: The continued effort at this height of struggling through the snow without snow-shoes (which the dogs have eaten), keeping the sledges upright, cursing one's dogs and continually restarting, tires one out almost beyond endurance.

And they still had a long way to go. It took another twelve days, fighting winds which sometimes blew at 208 kilometres an hour, before they began to search for the Union Jack which indicated where the ice cap station lay buried beneath the snow. They were eventually forced to pitch tents and crawl, half-frozen, into their sleeping bags.

2 December: It was freezing over sixty degrees and the wind bit through our clothes as if we were naked.

It was not until after dark on the next day, in eighty degrees of frost, that they spotted the Union Jack. The joyous reunion with the two members of the ice cap station, 'Doc' Bingham and Jimmy D'Aeth, was dampened for Courtauld by the intense pain of frost-bite in his toes and fingers. On 4 December, Bingham, a doctor, wrote in his own journal: "Courtauld wants to stay alone, but I have given a very decided opinion against it."

4 December: Doc and the others do not like the idea of my staying here alone, as it may be for three or four months, but short of abandoning the station there is no alternative as there is only food for one man for that period.

On 5 December, expedition leader Freddie Chapman commented: "The Doctor and D'Aeth are dead against one man staying alone. They say they have experienced it and they know. However, Courtauld is determined to stay, and eventually we gave in. Courtauld is very keen to stay, and judging by . . . experience among the Labrador trappers it is not so bad as people make out."

On the 6 December, Courtauld said goodbye to the others:

I took a photo, and then with a 'Damma, damma, damma'[1] they were away down the trail. Now I am quite alone. Not a dog or even a mosquito for company. There is nothing to complain of unless it be the curse of having to go out every three hours into the cold wind to observe the weather.

And so he settled into a life of cold solitude with enough

1 Eskimo cry used for urging on sledge dogs

food to last him, reasonably comfortably, for three months. By careful rationing he knew he could last for four months without much discomfort. As it happened, gale-force snow storms completely buried the reserves of food which had been stored outside his ice cap home, and it was to be five months before Courtauld, by then without food or fuel, was to see his friends again.

His ice cap home consisted of a 2.5 metre-high snow wall circling a tent connected by access tunnels to two snow houses, or igloos. It was primitive to say the least. The snow-buried umbrella-shaped tent, reached by a 6-metre crawl-through tunnel which entered through the floor, had a length of brass tubing projecting up through the crust of snow and ice for ventilation. There were two raised 'divans' made from boxes, a skin-covered floor, a 'galley' box with a primus stove and lamp, empty tins for rubbish, and a number of storage lockers made from boxes. The snow-house igloos, reached by side-branches from the main tunnel, provided additional space for storing food and the vital supplies of paraffin on which Courtauld was dependent for both heating and cooking. Boxes of food were buried in the snow just outside the entrance. His lavatory was a deep ice closet dug into the snow with a sledge stretched across it for a seat.

9 December: Nothing of note today except that I changed my underclothes as I had had itching for the last night or two. Found a good many bugs, much to my disgust, so put my clothes out in the snow in the pious hope that the cold would kill them.

16 December: Tonight unbandaged toes. Unpleasant

sight. Left toenail came off. Others will soon, I expect.

As Christmas approached he was to write in his diary:

At ten o'clock it was completely still. The silence was almost terrible. Nothing to hear but one's heart beating and the blood ticking in one's veins . . . Other toenail came off tonight. Looks very nasty, all soft, dead and gooing.

31 December: New Year's Eve! It is certainly quiet. The last few days, have been fine and cool with some magnificent aurorae.[1] Toes have been hurting considerably lately, so bathed and bandaged them.
N.Y. Resolutions
1. Mend moccasins and sleeping bag.
2. Get home and ask M. to marry me.
3. Find (a) a house (Suffolk, Sussex, or Dorset); (b) a boat; (c) a job. (a) and (b) rather depend on condition of financial affairs when I get home.
4. Give up exploring.
5. Collect a library and study (a) English literature and poetry; (b) Music; (c) Polar expoloration with a view possibly to try to write a book about it.

Four days later there was so much snow, and the wind blew so hard, that Courtauld spent the entire morning, and half the afternoon, trying to dig his way out through

---

1 The Northern, or Southern, lights – a luminous atmospheric phenomenon, like a natural and magnificent firework display in the sky, occuring near the earth's northern or southern magnetic poles.

the tunnel entrance. Late in the afternoon, exhausted, he retired to the tent, resigned to being entombed.

1 February: I wonder when, if ever, I shall get away from here. Not that I am bored, but I notice that my legs are getting very thin, partly from want of exercise and partly from lack of fresh food, I suppose. If I have to sledge back it will be pretty rotten unless the going is good enough to ride. These gales are nerve-racking things. I am daily expecting the house to fall in, for both the side snow-houses have partly done so.

14 February: Have now been ten weeks alone. Only one more day's food after today.

26 February: Am down to the last four gallons of paraffin now. If the others don't turn up in three or four weeks, I shall be reduced to cold and darkness. If I ever get back to the Base nothing will induce me to go on the ice cap again. When the others will come God knows.

15 March: Less than two gallons of paraffin left now. Hope to goodness the others come before it runs out or I shall have nothing to drink.

5 April: Now been here alone four months. No sign of relief. Only about a cupful of paraffin left and one or two candles. Have to lie in darkness almost all the time. But I trust in God absolutely. I am sure He does not mean me to die alone here . . .

20 April: Only one candle left. Hardly any paraffin. Lie in dark all day . . . Left foot swelling up, hope it isn't scurvy.

26 April: Just six months since we left Base and started living on sledge rations. Been here about twenty weeks. Everything running out. Using last candle. Very little paraffin. What I shall do for drinking water I don't know.

1 May: No sign of relief. Shall have to think of walking soon if I can get out. Am burning ski-wax for light, but it makes mostly smoke. Lemon juice is running low, which is pretty serious.[1]

6 May: Yesterday was the greatest day of my life . . . The primus gave its last gasp as I was melting water. Had just decided that I should have to start and walk back on June 1st if I could get out, when suddenly there was an appalling noise like a bus going by, followed by a confused yelling noise. I nearly jumped out of my skin. Was it the house falling in at last? A second later I realized the truth. It was somebody, some real human voice, calling down the ventilator. It was a wonderful moment. I could not think what to do or say. I yelled back some stuttering remarks that seemed quite futile for the occasion. "Hooray," they shouted. "Are you all right?" "Yes, thank God you've come. I am perfectly fit." "Thank God," they said. It was Gi [Watkins – expedition leader] and Freddie [Chapman]. They were as relieved as I was. The whole world seemed turned inside out. At one moment I was lying in the dark

1 Explorers frequently rely on regular consumption of lemon juice as a prevention against scurvy, a disease resulting from a deficiency of vitamin C. Scurvy causes general bodily weakness, extreme tenderness of the gums, pains in the limbs, and eventually death.

wondering how ever I was going to see anybody again or ever get home, and the next, home was in sight . . .

The diary entry for 6 May was made while Courtauld lay comfortably propped among sleeping bags as a team of dogs pulled his sledge on the first stage of the journey back to base. The previous night he had spent in a dry, warm tent, with a roaring primus, food and light. He could eat very little, and did not try. Nor could he sleep, for excitement.

The journey back took five days. Courtauld was able to ride all the way, reading and joking with his friends as the sledge slipped over dazzling white snow beneath a burning blue sky.

"It is very like sailing across a dead white sea," he wrote later. "Once I get to Base I shall stay there. I have had enough of sledging, ice caps and boat journeys."

But he hadn't. Just a month later he set out, with two companions, on an epic open-boat voyage of 600 miles, down the east coast and round the tip of Greenland. He reached England in November. He married and in 1934 returned with his wife to the icy wastes of Greenland.

The Survivalist's Handbook

Chapter 6:

Emergencies and First Aid

It's always a good idea to be prepared for emergency situations that could happen when you're not within easy reach of a telephone to call the emergency services. If you can arrange to get some professional first aid training, you may one day be able to save an injured person's life out in the wild. Most accidents, however, happen in the home or on the roads, so you *could* find yourself in a survival situation at any time, probably when you're least expecting it.

1.   Accidents of all kinds can often put the rescuer at risk. Always take great care at the scene of an accident, and never put yourself in danger unless you are completely confident of your own abilities.

2.   Be sure to alert the emergency services straight away if you see an accident or fire. Ambulance men and women, firefighters and the police are specially trained to deal with these situations, and often the best action you can take is to contact them immediately, stay calm and be on hand to help them if they ask you to. If it's impossible to contact the emergency services, don't attempt any first aid yourself unless you are

absolutely sure that you know what you're doing – it's better to concentrate on getting help.

3. If you're planning a trip in the wild, remember to pack a first aid kit. This should include sticking-plasters, gauze dressing, bandages (including a large one that could be used as a sling), safety pins, antiseptic lotion, some aspirin tablets and a pair of scissors.

4. Take a first aid course to learn how to put an injured person into the recovery position, and to learn about artificial ventilation and resucitation. But you should never move anyone if you're not sure what their injuries are – moving someone who has hurt their back could make the injury worse.

5. If someone gets burnt, the best thing is to get the burn into some cold water straight away, and leave it there until the skin is cool. Cover the burn with a light bandage to prevent infection.

6. You can easily get sunstroke if you don't cover yourself up properly in the sun, or if you over-exert yourself in the sun. The result is very unpleasant, and causes sickness, fever and headaches. Make sure anyone suffering from sunstroke gets into the shade, and keep them as cool as possible – but never hose them with cold water or use ice, as they could go into shock.

7. If someone is bitten by an animal, it's very important to clean the wound thoroughly to prevent infection from bacteria in the animal's mouth. Use clean water and rinse the wound for as long as possible to make sure it's well cleaned. Use antiseptic lotion if you have some and cover the wound with a sterile dressing.

8. Before modern medicines, people used natural resources to cure various complaints. You might have heard that a dock leaf rubbed over a nettle sting will help to reduce the pain – and it works! Spagnum moss was used as recently as the First World War as a dressing for cuts. Various types of fungus and herbs used to be used as dressings and medicines. The fungus crampball can be left to smoulder at the edge of a camp fire to drive away mosquitos.

The Will
to Survive –
Against All Odds

D o you think you could have survived alone in the arctic wastes, like Augustine Courtauld? Or made it through the dangers and burning heat of the African jungle, like Leoncio Bravo Salavador? A good knowledge of survival techniques is helpful, but even more important are courage and determination . . .

1.   Stranded alone in the Libyan desert, an SAS officer managed to walk 225 kilometres to the nearest water-hole. He had no supplies apart from a compass, some matches, and just two pints of salty water. All survival guides will tell you never to drink your own urine, but this officer broke the rules in desperation, and lived to tell the tale. He eventually made it to the water-hole, where he was rescued by a passing jeep. Amazingly, within a month he was back working with his unit.

2.   Alain Bombard, a 26-year-old French doctor, intentionally set himself adrift on a tiny raft in the Atlantic ocean because he wanted to prove that it is possible to survive by drinking sea water and catching food from the sea. He ate fish speared with a home-made harpoon, plankton for its Vitamin C, and drank rain water and sea water. He expected to reach the West Indies in about 30 days, but after more than six weeks at sea he was picked up by a British ship, still 1,130 kilometres from land. Alain took a shower and a light meal on board the ship, then, with an amazing effort of will, got back on to his raft to face another 1,130 kilometres alone on the ocean. Two weeks later he arrived in Barbados. He had survived his self-imposed ordeal but, sadly, never recovered his full health.

3.   New born babies were pulled alive from beneath the rubble of a Mexican hospital after it was demolished by an earthquake. The babies had been buried for nine days under tons of concrete and masonry, protected only by their cots and the bedding they were wrapped in. They were, of course, dreadfully weak and desperately hungry; but they lived.

4.   Jackie Greaves, a woman of 51, suffered a terrifying ordeal when she was lost for 40 hours in the snow and ice of Scotland's Caringorm mountains during the harsh British winter of 1993. Jackie knew exactly what to do. She survived by digging herself a snow-hole and staying put, comparatively warm and well sheltered, until she heard the voices of her rescuers.

5.   In the scorching heat of the Mexican desert, a man became lost, miles from anywhere and with very little water. Over eight days, he travelled 217 kilometres to safety, having survived on just two pints of water a day. When he was found, his flesh was burned black, his lips, nose and eyelids had shrunk to nothing, and he had lost a quarter of his original weight. He eventually returned to perfect health – although his hair had turned completely grey!

6.   Lauren Elder found herself the only survivor of a plane crash in the Sierra Nevada mountains of California. Lauren was badly injured, with a broken arm and a terrible gash on her leg, and cut and frost-bitten feet. Despite her condition, she managed to climb 2,500 metres down the sheer face of the mountain, fight her way

through forest wilderness, and trudge for a day and a night across the Owens Valley Desert, before she was finally rescued.

T R U E HORROR ST O RIES

Incredible? Impossible? Too awful to imagine? But someone, somewhere, at some time has sworn that each of these strange stories is true . . .

A girl murders her own father and mother in cold blood.

A whole village of people disappears without trace, and all anyone saw were strange lights in the sky.

An Egyptian mummy, disturbed after thousands of years, leaves a trail of horrible disasters.

Some of these stories have possible explanations, but for others there is *no* answer. Consider the facts and decide for yourself whether each gruesome story really is true – but keep the cover firmly closed once darkness falls, or your dreams could turn into NIGHTMARES . . .

T R U E
MONSTER
STORIES

Incredible? Impossible? Too awful to imagine? But someone, somewhere, at some time has sworn that each of these strange stories is true . . .

A newspaper reports of a monster man, whose fiery breath scorched the faces of his victims.

An American swears to his dying day, he was kidnapped by a family of Bigfoot or ape men.

And centuries old records tell of a beached sea monster so huge, a man could be drowned inside it.

Read accounts of the Yeti, the vampire, and less well-known beasts, like Black Dog and Morgawr; consider the facts and decide for yourself whether these monster stories really are true. And even if you choose not to believe, beware! These tales may linger in your thoughts and darken your dreams . . .

TRUE CRIME STORIES

Nine compelling crime stories full of suspense, daring and intrigue . . . and each one is true!

A terrifying siege ends when two brave citizens bring the infamous Ned Kelly to justice at last.

A bloody clue under the floor helps an ingenious detective to identify a brutal murderer.

A game of Monopoly played with real money helps expose the Great Train Robbers.

Highwaymen, pirates, murderers, kidnappers; with this gruesome collection of gripping real-life crime stories, you can be caught up in the thrills and danger of crime within the comfort and safety of your own armchair.

T R U E

SPORT

ST O RIES

Over eighty incredible facts that have hit the sporting headlines and eight gripping stories that reveal the drama behind the news.

Read about:

Muhammad Ali's amazing rise to boxing fame.

Swimmer Dawn Fraser's struggle against all odds to achieve record-breaking success.

How Eddie the Eagle came last in the Olympic ski-jump and still emerged a national hero!

Sometimes hilarious, sometimes heart-breaking, often surprising – True Sport Stories has something for everyone.